From Work to School

PIONEER EDITION

By Shirleyann Costigan

CONTENTS

2 From Work to School

8 From Work to School Around the World

10 The Photographs That Changed the Nation

12 Concept Check

From Work to School

By Shirleyann Costigan

Boys work on machines
in a factory.

What does "work" mean to you?

Maybe it means doing a few chores around the house. Clean your room. Take out the trash. Feed the cat. Maybe it means a dollar allowance for your pocket. Whatever it means to you, work isn't always fun. Sometimes you don't want to do it.

Yet children in America have always worked. Children worked in the fields, in shops, and in **factories**. The work was not always bad for them, but sometimes it was. Many children worked long hours for little or no **pay**. Sometimes the work made them sick. This kind of work is called "child labor."

Today, there are laws in America that **protect** children who work. It may be difficult to believe, but these laws did not always exist in America. In those days, childhood was different than it is today.

A Changing America

Two hundred years ago, life in America was different than today. Most people lived on farms or in small towns. Most children worked. They helped out in the fields. They helped out with chores in the home.

Then, new machines were invented. The machines worked better and faster than people. Many people lost their jobs. They moved to cities to find work. **Employers** hired whole families to work for them. They even hired children.

This girl helps pick potatoes.

4

Teenage boys work in a cotton factory.

Fursen Owens, age twelve

Children at Work

Some children worked twelve to eighteen hours a day, six days a week. Children never earned much money. Older children could earn a dollar a week. Children from three to five years old earned only pennies a day. The children gave every penny to their families to buy food or to pay for the rent.

Some of the older children were allowed to attend school. But usually they were too tired to learn. They had no time to study. Many children didn't attend school at all.

Fursen Owens was twelve. He had already worked for four years. He couldn't read or write. "Yes, I want to learn," he said, "but I can't when I work all the time."

Children worked in factories, mills, coal mines, canneries, and sold newspapers on the streets. Small children worked at home. They sewed buttons on garments for clothing companies. When brothers and sisters came home from school, they would work, too. These children did not have much chance to get a good education.

Children stand outside a common school.

Two girls go to school.

School and Play

When most people lived on farms, children went to school only when they weren't working in the fields. The schools they attended were called common schools. A common school had one room. Students from six to sixteen studied in the same room. One teacher taught all of them. Students had no books. They had no pencils or paper. They wrote their lessons on a slate with a piece of chalk.

When farm children were not in school, they helped out at home. Farm and household chores had to be done everyday. Toys were simple and handmade. Books were rare and were read by candlelight.

Public Schools and Parks

By 1900, many things had changed in the United States. Inventions like electricity made life easier. More and more people lived and worked in cities.

People began to worry about children who worked. Many people knew that this wasn't right.

Wordwise

employer: person or company that you work for

factory: large building where people use machines to make goods

pay: money that your employer gives you for work you have done

protect: to keep someone or something safe from harm or damage

6

They knew that time to play and go to school would make children better citizens. They thought school would make children better workers, too. They wanted children to work less and go to school more.

At the same time, new public schools replaced the old common schools. These public schools were like the schools most children attend today. Students were separated by their ages into grades. Each grade had its own classroom. More books were available. Students still used a slate and chalk. Discipline was very strict. Children didn't dare fool around in school.

There were also new public parks and city playgrounds where children could play. Machine-made toys became popular. Model trains, teddy bears, crayons, and bikes were favorite toys.

Organizations looked out for children, too. The Young Men's Christian Association (YMCA) opened gyms. It gave swimming lessons for free. The Boy Scouts of America began in 1910. Girl Scouts and other scout groups soon followed. These organizations taught young people how to be responsible adults.

Finally, in 1938, the U.S. Congress passed fair labor laws. The laws limited the number of hours a child could work. They made employers pay children at least twenty-five cents an hour. Children were not allowed to work in unhealthy places. Soon, fewer children were working full-time. More children started to attend school. By that time, all children between the ages of eight and fourteen had to go to school. These laws continue to protect children in the U.S. today.

Boys play a game with marbles.

From Work to School
AROUND THE WORLD

Sadly, children in other countries are not always protected. Many work long hours for little or no pay. But organizations, caring adults, and even children are helping to change this.

"The bravest voice can live in the smallest body." That's what Craig Kielburger learned when he read about a boy named Iqbal Masih. Iqbal worked for a cruel employer for many years. When Iqbal got older, he left the factory. He told people about his life as a child worker. He was killed for telling his story.

Craig wanted to help children like Iqbal. He and his friends wrote to world leaders about working children. They raised money at garage sales, car washes, and bake sales. They asked for donations. The money helped to build schools and shelters for child workers.

Craig named his organization Free the Children. It's the world's largest group of children helping children.

Craig knows that education is the key to a better life. Educated children grow up to be better adults. They find better jobs. When all children go to school instead of to work, then child labor will stop for good.

Craig Kielburger and a student

The Photographs That

Lewis Hine was a New York City schoolteacher and photographer. His photographs of child workers in the early 1900s shocked the nation. They helped people see why they needed to make stronger laws against child labor.

Lewis Hine took this picture of Michael NcNelis. He was eight. Michael was found selling newspapers during a rainstorm. He had just recovered from pneumonia.

Newsboys were called "newsies." In those days, they made about thirty cents a day.

In 1899, thousands of newsboys went on strike for more money.

One of the strikers was called Kid Blink because he was blind in one eye. He spoke to the newies.

"Friens and feller workers. Dis is a time which tries de hearts of men. Dis is de time when we'se got to stick together like glue.... We know wot we wants and we'll git it even if we is blind."

—*"NEWSIE" KID BLINK*

Changed the Nation

This girl was fifty-one inches high and had been working in the mill one year. Sometimes she worked at night. She managed four machines for forty-eight cents a day.

When Lewis Hine asked this girl how old she was, she said, "I don't remember. I'm not old enough to work, but do just the same."

Children and parents often lied about a child's age to get a job. Children under ten years old often worked twelve hours a day.

In the seafood industry, children worked with sharp knives. They constantly cut their fingers. "The salt water gets into the cuts and they ache," said one boy. It was a smelly job, too.

School Rules!

Find out about children moving from work to school. Then answer these questions.

1 List one way that America changed between the 1800s and the 1900s.

2 What kinds of work did children do on farms? What changed when they started to work in factories?

3 How were common schools different from public schools?

4 How did the labor laws of 1938 help protect child workers?

5 How are the author's viewpoints about Iqbal on page 8 and the "newsies" on page 10 alike? How are they different?